5 STEPS TO DRAWING
FARM ANIMALS

by Pamela Hall • illustrated by Sharon Lane Holm

Published by The Child's World®
1980 Lookout Drive • Mankato, MN 56003-1705
800-599-READ • www.childsworld.com

ACKNOWLEDGMENTS
The Child's World®: Mary Berendes, Publishing Director
The Design Lab: Design and production
Red Line Editorial: Editorial direction

ISBN: 978-1-60973-199-1
LCCN: 2011927708

Printed in the United States of America
Mankato, MN
July 2011
PA02088

TABLE OF CONTENTS

WHAT ARE FARM ANIMALS FOR?

Baa, quack, oink, moo. Who makes these sounds? Farm animals do!

Many farms raise animals. Most farms raise **livestock** for food. Cows and horses often eat in **pastures** in the warmer months. Farmers keep and feed them inside when it is cold. Food is kept in **bulk feeders**, which keep it clean and dry. The animals eat from these feeders. The food is brought down to the animals when it is time to eat.

Livestock give us meat, eggs, and milk. They give us other goods, too. The skin from cows is made into leather. The wool of sheep is made into blankets or clothes. The hooves and horns can be made into buttons, combs, and glue. **Manure** from these animals helps crops grow.

We couldn't live without farms. Almost all the meat we eat comes from farm animals.

FARM LIFE

Farmers are busy all day long. They make sure everything runs smoothly. Each type of animal needs a different place to live. Cows and horses stay in stalls. Rabbits live in hutches. Chickens sleep in coops and walk in the yard. Farmers must make sure these places are safe so their animals don't stray. These places must be kept clean, too.

Each animal needs a different type of food. All animals must have fresh water, and they must have medicine when they get sick. Sometimes farmers even help the animals have their babies.

Farm animals can be very helpful on a farm. Sheep eat the weeds out of pastures. Horses can help herd cattle.

HOW FARMING HAS CHANGED

Years ago, most people farmed to make a living. In the 1800s, most farms in the United States were small family farms. A farm family would raise many different types of crops and animals. Today, family farms are much bigger. They are run like businesses. But farmers still care for their animals.

Now, most farmers raise just one kind of crop or animal. The chores depend on the type of crop grown or animal raised. On dairy farms, cows are raised to make milk and milk goods. Farm work starts when it is still dark outside. Equipment is cleaned. Cows must be fed and milked two or three times each day. Milk goes right from the cow into a refrigerated truck.

DRAWING TIPS

You've learned about farm animals. You're almost ready to draw them. But first, here are a few drawing tips:

Every artist needs tools. To learn how to draw farm animals, you will need:

- Some paper
- A pencil
- An eraser
- Markers, crayons, colored pencils, or watercolors (optional)

Anyone can learn to draw. You might think only some people can draw. That's not true. Everyone can learn to draw. It takes practice, though. The more you draw, the better you will be. With practice, you will become a true artist!

Everyone makes mistakes. This is okay! Mistakes help you learn. They help you know what not to do next time. Mistakes can even make your drawing more special. It's all right if you draw the pig's belly too big. Now you've got a one-of-a-kind drawing. You can erase a mistake you don't like, too. Then start again!

Stay loose. Relax your body before you begin. Hold your pencil lightly. Don't rest your wrist on the table. Instead, move your whole arm as you draw. This will help you make smooth lines. Press lightly on the paper when you draw or erase.

Drawing is fun! The most important thing about drawing is to have fun. Be creative. Your drawings don't have to look exactly like the pictures in this book. Try changing the position of the horse or the spots on the cow. You can also use markers, crayons, colored pencils, or watercolors to bring your farm animals to life.

COW

Cows have a great sense of smell. They can smell up to 5 miles (8 km) away. They communicate with one another by mooing. No two cows have the same pattern of spots.

SHEEP

14

Sheep can eat on the hilliest, rockiest land. They make great lawn mowers by eating grass and weeds. We get wool from their thick, fleecy coats. Lanolin is a natural oil found in sheep's fleece. We use lanolin to make candle wax.

5

PIG

16

Pigs are the fourth most intelligent animals in the world. They do not really "eat like pigs." They actually eat their food slowly.

5

CHICKEN

18

There are more than 60 types of chickens. All chickens have wings. But they can only fly short distances. They fly mostly to escape enemies. However, they are fast runners. They can run up to 9 miles per hour (14.5 km/h).

5

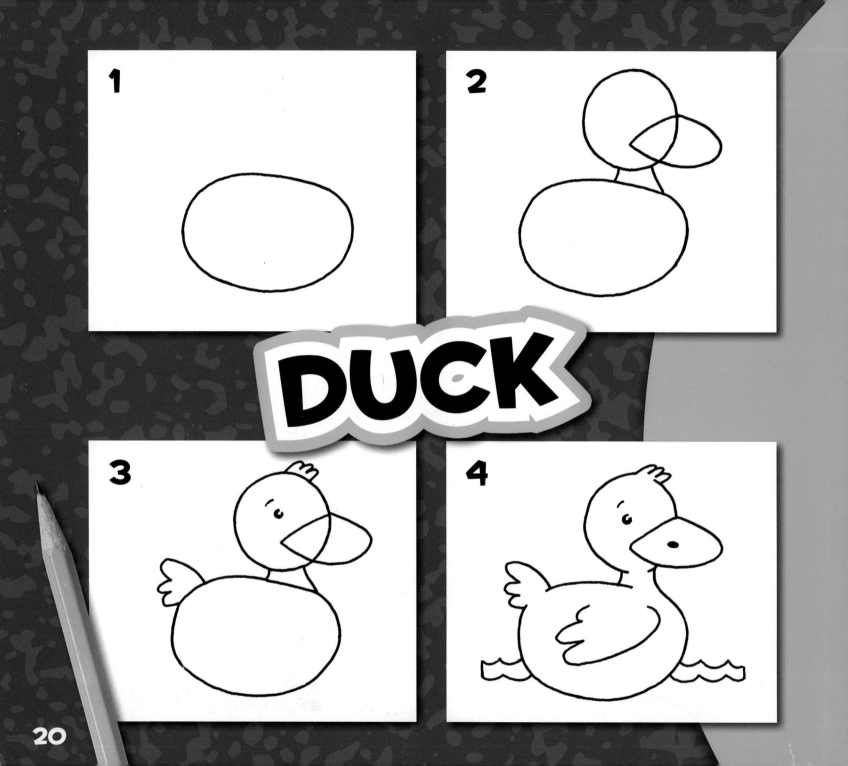

1

2

DUCK

3

4

Ducks have webbed feet that act like canoe paddles. Their feet push them through the water. Ducks have waterproof feathers on top. They have soft, downy feathers underneath. These feathers keep them warm.

5

GOAT

Goats provide us with milk. More people in the world drink goat's milk than cow's milk. Goats smell their food to make sure it is clean and tasty.

1

2

RABBIT

3

4

24

Rabbits like to eat roots, grasses, and plants with their long front teeth. They love to run and jump with their strong back legs.

5

1

2

HORSE

3

4

Horses are beautiful creatures. They have strong bodies and long, lean legs. Horses like to eat hay, carrots, apples, and roots. They eat about 15 to 20 pounds (6.8–9 kg) of food every day!

MORE DRAWING

Now you know how to draw farm animals. Here are some ways to keep drawing them.

Farm animals come in all different colors, shapes, sizes, and textures. You can draw them all! Try using pens or colored pencils to draw and color in details. Experiment with crayons and markers to give your drawings different colors and textures. You can also paint your drawings. Watercolors are easy to use. If you make a mistake, you can wipe it away with a damp cloth. Try tracing the outline of your drawing with a crayon or a marker. Then paint over it with watercolor. What happens?

Drawing Real Farm Animals

When you want something new to draw, just look around. Can you find a picture of a farm animal? Maybe you can take a field trip to a farm and see the animals in person. Then, try drawing the animals. First, look at one animal carefully. Is it big or small? What color is it? Does it have long fur or no fur at all? Does it have spots? How long is its tail? Now try drawing it! If you need help, use the examples in this book to guide you.

GLOSSARY

bulk feeders (BULK FEE-durs): Bulk feeders are containers used to store large amounts of food. Bulk feeders store and release grain this is used to feed farm animals.

livestock (LYV-stok): Livestock are animals that are raised for food or money. Livestock include cows and pigs.

manure (muh-NOO-ur): Manure is animal feces that are used as a fertilizer to help plants grow. Some manure comes from farm animals.

pastures (PASS-churs): Pastures are lands covered with plants and grasses used for feeding livestock. Cows feed on pastures.

FIND OUT MORE

BOOKS

Emberley, Ed. *Ed Emberley's Drawing Book: Make a World*. New York: Little Brown, 2006.

Gravel, Elise. *Let's Draw and Doodle Together*. Maplewood, NJ: Blue Apple Books, 2010.

Torres, Jickie. *Learn to Draw Farm Animals*. Minneapolis, MN: Walter Foster, 2011.

WEB SITES

Visit our Web site for links about drawing farm animals:

childsworld.com/links

Note to Parents, Teachers, and Librarians: We routinely verify our Web links to make sure they are safe and active sites. So encourage your readers to check them out!

INDEX

ABOUT THE AUTHOR:
Pamela Hall lives near the St. Croix River in Lakeland, Minnesota, with her children and dog. Along with writing for children, Pamela enjoys being outdoors and feeding wildlife.

ABOUT THE ILLUSTRATOR:
Sharon Lane Holm has been drawing pictures her entire life. She has been a children's book illustrator for many years. Sharon lives in New Fairfield, Connecticut. She paints with fluid acrylics and adds colored pencil.